Americana

STATE FAIRS
THEN AND NOW

Abdo & Daughters
MIDDLE GRADE NONFICTION
An Imprint of Abdo Publishing
abdobooks.com

Jessica Rusick

ABDOBOOKS.COM

Published by Abdo Publishing, a division of ABDO, PO Box 398166, Minneapolis, Minnesota 55439. Copyright © 2024 by Abdo Consulting Group, Inc. International copyrights reserved in all countries. No part of this book may be reproduced in any form without written permission from the publisher. Abdo & Daughters™ is a trademark and logo of Abdo Publishing.

Printed in the United States of America, North Mankato, Minnesota

102023

012024

THIS BOOK CONTAINS RECYCLED MATERIALS

Design: Kelly Doudna, Mighty Media, Inc.

Production: Denise Hamernik, Mighty Media, Inc.

Editor: Liz Salzmann

Cover Photographs: Shutterstock Images (bottom), Wikimedia Commons (top)

Interior Photographs: Adobe Stock, p. 45 (bottom); AP Images, pp. 4–5; Flickr, pp. 32, 35, 36 (left), 37 (bottom); iStockphoto, p. 40; Library of Congress, pp. 10, 12, 16–17, 45 (top); Mighty Media, Inc., pp. 3, 41, 42–43; Shutterstock Images, pp. 1 (bottom), 6, 7, 8–9, 13, 14–15, 18, 19, 20–21, 22–23, 24, 25, 26, 27, 28, 30–31, 34, 36 (right), 36–37 (map), 38–39; Wikimedia Commons, pp. 1 (top), 11, 29, 33, 37 (top), 44 (both)

Design Elements: iStockphoto, Shutterstock

LIBRARY OF CONGRESS CONTROL NUMBER: 2023939348

PUBLISHER'S CATALOGING-IN-PUBLICATION DATA

Names: Rusick, Jessica, author.

Title: State fairs: then and now / by Jessica Rusick

Other title: then and now

Description: Minneapolis, Minnesota : Abdo Publishing, 2024 | Series: Americana | Includes online resources and index.

Identifiers: ISBN 9781098291785 (lib. bdg.) | ISBN 9781098278687 (ebook)

Subjects: LCSH: Americana--Juvenile literature. | Agricultural exhibitions--Juvenile literature. | State fairs--Juvenile literature. | History, Modern--Juvenile literature.

Classification: DDC 973.0--dc23

TABLE OF CONTENTS

A State Fair Tradition 5

Early State Fairs 9

State Fair Entertainment 17

State Fair Farming and Exhibits 23

State Fair Food 31

What's Next? 39

Make Americana! 42

Timeline 44

Glossary 46

Online Resources 47

Index 48

The butter sculptures at the Ohio State Fair are different each year. In 2014, they included the Ohio state symbols.

Chapter 1

A STATE FAIR TRADITION

It is a warm and muggy summer day at the 2022 Ohio State Fair. Hundreds of fairgoers crowd inside the Dairy Products Building. They press forward to get a glimpse of ten sculptures. One sculpture is a smiling child holding the reins of a calf. Another is a farmer with a chicken in his arms. The display honors Ohio's agricultural history. The sculptures are kept behind glass at temperatures nearly as cold as a refrigerator. That's because they are made of butter!

Butter sculptures first debuted at the Ohio State Fair nearly 120 years earlier, in 1903. Since then, the sculptures have become a beloved state fair tradition in Ohio and other states. In Ohio, nearly 500,000 guests will visit the butter sculptures during the 12-day state fair.

The butter sculptures are just one attraction at the Ohio State Fair. A midway boasts colorful rides and carnival games. Large buildings showcase different farm animals and the products they produce. Other buildings feature handmade items such as knitted clothing, baked goods, and paintings. Food stands dot the wide, paved avenues. Later that night, thousands of people will gather for a rock concert at the concert hall.

What Are State Fairs?

State fairs are yearly festivals usually held in late summer or early fall. They take place at large fairgrounds with permanent buildings. Nearly every state in the United States has a state fair. Some states have more than one! State fairs feature agricultural displays, food stands, rides, concerts, shopping, and many other attractions. Contests are held for the best farm animals, baked goods, artwork, and more.

The Ohio State Fair is held from late July to early August in Columbus, Ohio.

The earliest American state fairs date back to the 1840s. These early fairs were largely attended by farmers. They came to display their finest animals and crops and to learn about new farming methods and technology. Modern state fairs are attended by people from many backgrounds. But the fairs are still places of learning. Farmers show the public how different crops are grown. Some state fairs also showcase advances in environmentally friendly technology. Most importantly, a state fair showcases what is special about the state. It allows people to take pride in local agriculture, art, and food. Each state fair also has its own unique, often wacky traditions. These lively fairs have become a beloved part of American culture.

Texas has four state fairs. One of them is held in Denton and features a rodeo.

The Minnesota State Fair is one of the most well-attended state fairs. An attendance record was set in 2019 when 2.1 million people went to the fair.

Chapter 2

EARLY STATE FAIRS

State fairs have their roots in ancient times. For thousands of years, people in countries around the world have gathered to display, buy, and sell food, livestock, and everyday items. Fairs have also been places to socialize, be entertained, and learn about advances in agriculture and technology.

The Rise of Commercial Agriculture

The growth of American state fairs is tied to the growth of American commercial farming. In the late 1700s, 90 percent of Americans were farmers. Most farms were small and family owned, producing enough crops to sustain one family. Only a small portion of farmers grew crops to sell at local markets.

In the late 1700s and early 1800s, the United States experienced the Industrial Revolution. This period was marked by new inventions and the growth of industry. New farming technology made it faster and easier to plant and harvest crops such as cotton and wheat. As a result, more American farmers began growing crops to sell.

At the same time, newly built mills and factories made it faster and easier to process crops into flour, textiles, and other goods. These changes in American life caused demand for crops to increase in the United States and abroad. Commercial farming quickly became an important part of the American economy.

The First American Fairs

As commercial farming increased, many communities believed it was important to promote and celebrate farming. American farmer Elkanah Watson pioneered the American agricultural fair for this purpose. In 1810, Watson organized a livestock show in Berkshire County, Massachusetts. Local farmers were encouraged to display their oxen, cattle, sheep, and pigs during the one-day fair. The exhibition was

One early farming innovation was the steel plow. It was invented by American blacksmith John Deere in 1837. Deere & Company went on to make other equipment including tractors and disc harrows (*pictured*).

a success! The fair attracted a large crowd of farmers and featured hundreds of animals.

The following year, Watson helped create the Berkshire Agricultural Society. Members included farmers, politicians, and other people who were interested in promoting agriculture. The society held a yearly agricultural fair in Berkshire County to promote improvements in farming methods.

Berkshire's 1811 fair featured many events that would later become common at state fairs. Farmers displayed livestock, crops, and homemade goods. Watson also helped nearby counties organize their own agricultural societies and fairs. By 1819, most counties in New England held an annual agricultural fair.

Before organizing the first agricultural fair, Elkanah Watson founded the State Bank of Albany in New York.

The First State Fair

Over the next decades, states outside New England established agricultural societies as well. The New York State Agricultural Society was founded in 1832. At first, it helped organize local county fairs. But in 1841, the society received money from the New York state legislature to launch America's first-ever state fair.

The two-day event was held in a field in Syracuse, New York. Farmers from all over the state gathered to showcase their crops and livestock. Educational displays also introduced farmers to new technology for the farm and home. Unlike modern state fairs, there were no permanent buildings or walkways. Displays were set up in large tents. Rain made the ground muddy and hard to walk on. Still, America's first state fair proved popular. Between 10,000 and 15,000 people attended.

In the 1920s, the Kentucky State Fair was held in a combination of tents and buildings.

Other Early State Fairs

Other states followed New York's example and held their own fairs. In 1849, Michigan became the second state to hold a state fair. The United States' territory expanded westward throughout the late 1800s. As it did, more areas became states and held state fairs. Iowa held its first state fair in 1854. Minnesota held its first state fair in 1859, just one year after becoming a state. Like the New York State Fair, these early fairs were held on temporary fairgrounds.

By modern standards, the state fairs were simple. Iowa's first state fair, for example, featured roughly 100 livestock, a large shed, a racetrack, and farm tool displays. The only entertainment was a horseback riding competition. Early state fairs generally lasted only a few days. The fairs ended at dusk each day because there were no streetlights at the temporary fairgrounds.

The Minnesota State Fair has been at its current St. Paul location since 1885.

The Importance of State Fairs

State fairs helped new states attract settlers. Showing off the crops and livestock a state could produce was a way to convince people to move to the area and farm. State fairs were important places of learning and discussion. Farmers could trade farming advice with each other. Local universities also presented their latest agricultural research. This included ways to increase crop yields and keep farm animals healthy.

In addition, farmers could purchase new equipment for their farms at the state fair. This included steam- or gasoline-powered plows, reapers, and tractors. And state fairs displayed more than just farming technology. They also showcased new technology for the home and for society in general. In the late

At modern state fairs, antique tractors and other equipment are often displayed to honor farming history.

1800s and early 1900s, many people were introduced to amazing discoveries and inventions such as electricity and airplanes at state fair displays and exhibitions.

In the 1930s, the Louisiana State Fair featured a drum corps parade. Today, there is a parade with various marching bands.

Chapter 3

STATE FAIR ENTERTAINMENT

Most early state fairs focused mainly on farming and education. But some featured other forms of entertainment. In 1849, the New York State Fair debuted a ride similar to a Ferris wheel. The hand-operated wooden wheel was 50 feet (15.2 m) tall. Four people at a time could ride it. It was popular among that year's 80,000 visitors. Early fairs also featured marching bands and horse shows.

Permanent Fairgrounds

Early state fairs changed locations every year or few years. But in the late 1800s and early 1900s, agricultural societies began to establish permanent fairgrounds. That way, the state fair could be held in the same place each year. It also meant fairgrounds could house livestock, exhibits, and goods in permanent buildings instead of tents. And it made the fair experience more comfortable for exhibitors and fairgoers alike.

Permanent fairgrounds covered hundreds of acres. Architects designed the fairgrounds to be inviting. They included paved paths, gardens, and streetlights. Permanent fairgrounds also often had large grandstands. Many modern state fairs hold concerts at the grandstands. Famous musicians and comedians perform for sold out audiences.

New Attractions

New fairgrounds allowed state fairs to expand in size, scope, and duration. State fair attractions grew in number. In the 1890s, the Iowa State Fair featured performances by trapeze artists and parachutists.

In addition to the state's annual fair, many fairgrounds host events, such as classic car shows, throughout the year.

In 1896, guests could even watch a staged train crash! Fair organizers laid train tracks at the grandstand and sent two train locomotives barreling into each other. This feat was repeated at the Iowa State Fair and at fairs across the country. Grandstand car races became common in the 1910s. By the 1920s, some state fairgrounds had large stages for concerts. They also had midways filled with carnival rides. In 1932, guests at the Wisconsin State Fair could take a blimp ride from the fairgrounds to the nearby lakefront!

Modern state fairs fill their schedules with shows, events, and activities to keep visitors entertained throughout each day.

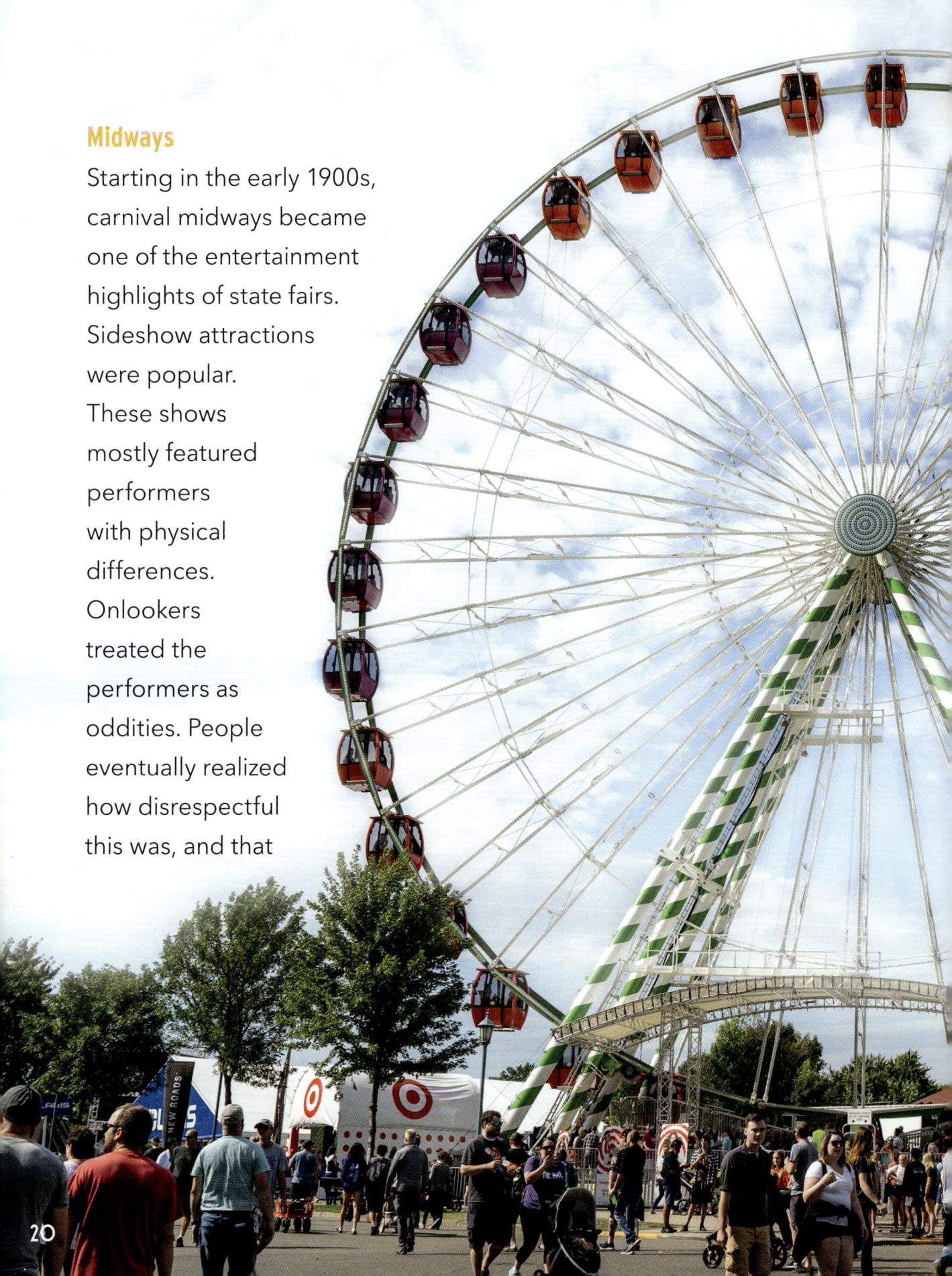

Midways

Starting in the early 1900s, carnival midways became one of the entertainment highlights of state fairs. Sideshow attractions were popular. These shows mostly featured performers with physical differences. Onlookers treated the performers as oddities. People eventually realized how disrespectful this was, and that

type of sideshow was discontinued. Modern state fair sideshows instead feature performers with incredible skills. These include jugglers and fire-eaters. Rides are the focus of most modern state fair midways. Midways in the early 1900s featured simple rides such as Ferris wheels and carousels. The tilt-a-whirl debuted at the Minnesota State Fair in 1926. Advances in technology have led to dozens of new carnival rides over the decades. Modern state fairs feature rides that can spin, flip, and soar!

> The Great Big Wheel has appeared at several state fairs, including the Minnesota State Fair (*pictured*). At 156 feet (47.5 m) high, it is one of the largest traveling Ferris wheels in North America.

The largest commercial farms in the United States range from about 80,000 to 190,000 acres (32,375 to 76,890 ha).

Chapter 4

STATE FAIR FARMING AND EXHIBITS

Farming remained a key part of state fairs even as they grew. Since the first state fair, however, the nature of American agriculture has changed dramatically. Also, more people were living in cities, so state fairs needed to appeal to farmers and nonfarmers alike.

From Rural to Urban

In the early 1900s, American farming started undergoing a huge shift. In 1900, about half of all Americans were farmers. Farming took place on small plots of land run by individual families. But over the next decades, farming equipment became more expensive. Many small farmers could no longer afford to run their farms.

At the same time, people moved from rural areas to urban ones for better job opportunities. In 1920, more Americans lived in urban areas than rural areas for the first time in history. This meant there were fewer farmers able to run family farms.

Many farmers sold their land to large, commercial farms. By 1940, only 30 percent of Americans lived on farms. This number continued to decrease over the next decades.

Farming at the State Fair

Most attendees at early state fairs were farmers. They came to state fairs to learn about the latest farming techniques. But since the 1930s, most fairgoers have been from urban and suburban areas. Many are unfamiliar with the ins and outs of farming. Still, farming and agriculture remain an important part of state fairs. Each state fair has buildings dedicated to different farm animals and industries. Visitors can walk through the buildings and see hundreds of farm animals. These include various breeds of horses, cows, sheep, and more.

State fairs award prizes to the best crops in many different categories.

Farmers teach visitors how crops are grown and how animals are bred. Attendees also learn how animal products such as milk and meat are produced on large farms. Fairgoers can watch cow-milking demonstrations or learn how yarn is spun. They can even watch farm animals being born!

Through these exhibitions, fairgoers can learn how farming plays a key role in their everyday lives. Some state fairs also showcase antique and modern farm equipment. Unlike past state fairs, however, farmers today do not attend the fair to purchase equipment. Modern farm implements are huge and cost thousands of dollars. Farmers generally order them from dealers or manufacturers. At modern fairs, some manufacturers sell smaller implements such as riding lawn mowers.

Farm equipment on display at the Missouri State Fair

State fairs are also still places where farmers can learn from each other. For example, modern farmers breed animals based on the newest genetic research. Farmers hope to raise animals that are healthy and produce high-quality milk, meat, or eggs. At state fairs, they can see how their breeding programs stack up against other farmers' programs. They can also win awards for their livestock.

Youth Agriculture

Youth programs are another important part of modern state fairs. These include organizations such as 4-H and Future Farmers of

The name 4-H reflects the organization's motto "head, heart, hands, and health." 4-H participants often work with animals during state fair shows and events.

America (FFA). 4-H was founded in the early 1900s. FFA was founded in 1928. These organizations promote leadership skills and agricultural knowledge in teens and young adults.

Members of 4-H and FFA work on projects throughout the year in their counties. They may raise a farm animal. Or they may conduct research projects in agricultural science or community health. The strongest projects are chosen for display at state fairs. Most 4-H and FFA members will not grow up to be farmers. But they may stay involved in agriculture as scientists, politicians, and community leaders.

Homemade Goods

Early state fairs were not just about farming. Women also displayed homemade goods, such as jam, pies, and quilts. The best homemade goods won prizes. Contests are still a huge part of modern state fairs. Now, both men and

Quilts are a common type of handwork shown at state fairs. At the Alaska State Fair (*pictured*), there are multiple categories and divisions for people to enter their quilts into.

women can submit their homemade goods. Participants submit their entries before the state fair begins. Crafters can also submit knitted items, weavings, woodwork, stamp collections, metalwork, canned foods, and more! There are dozens of categories for baked goods alone. These include different types of breads, pies, cookies, and cakes. Judges review the entries. Then they award ribbons of different colors to the best ones. At many state fairs, the first-place ribbons are blue.

The New York State Fair Energy and Environment Experience included information about renewable energy, such as wind energy.

Eco-Friendly Additions

Since their inception, state fairs have been places to learn about new technology. In modern times, many state fairs also teach about conservation and the environment. In 2006, the Eco Experience building opened at the Minnesota State Fair. It teaches people about sustainability and eco-friendly technology. The building has featured displays on wind energy, electronics recycling, and water pollution. Interactive exhibits teach visitors how they can go green in their everyday lives. In 2022, the Energy and Environment Experience opened at the New York State Fair. Hands-on exhibits teach fairgoers about charging electric vehicles and how to conserve energy at home.

In 2012, the Eco Experience at the Minnesota State Fair included the Bottle Buyology exhibit that encouraged people to recycle more. It featured a large tunnel made of discarded plastic bottles to show how many plastic bottles are thrown away.

Modern state fairs often have food buildings where vendors sell many different kinds of food.

Chapter 5

STATE FAIR FOOD

Food is another important and popular part of the state fair experience. State fair food has changed dramatically over time. In the 1800s, many fairgrounds had tented dining halls. They were run by local churches. Volunteers from the churches cooked large batches of food to serve at a noon meal. The meal often included home-cooked staples such as meatloaf and mashed potatoes. Fairgoers ate together at long tables. Eating at a dining hall became an early state fair tradition.

In the late 1800s and early 1900s, church dining halls moved into permanent buildings. At some state fairs, these dining halls continued to operate into the 2020s. The meals were no longer served at a set time and there were many more food options available. But fairgoers could still enjoy eating together at long, communal tables.

Food Stands

As state fairs expanded in the 1900s, state fair food began to change. There were now more attractions to see. So fairgoers wanted food that they could eat as they walked around. Vendors sold food that was easy to make and easy for fairgoers to eat while walking. Popular foods included popcorn, peanuts, and hot dogs. Vendors sold them from food stands and food carts.

This food revolution paved the way for classic state fair staples. Cotton candy debuted in 1904 at the St. Louis World's Fair and soon

One of the state fairs with the most food vendors is the Iowa State Fair. It has about 200 food booths each year.

appeared at state fairs. The corn dog made its state fair debut in Texas in 1942. These foods were served on sticks, which made them ideal for eating on the go. Tom Thumb mini donuts debuted in 1949 at the Minnesota State Fair. Since then, mini donuts have become popular at other Midwestern state fairs.

Food stands are a staple of modern state fairs. Many are housed in permanent buildings or booths. Some have been run by the same families for generations!

New Offerings

Modern state fair food has grown in variety. Each year, state fair food vendors develop creative and wacky new recipes to attract fairgoers to their stands. Many foods are deep-fried and served on a stick. In

There are so many different creative food items at the State Fair of Texas, they have the Big Tex Choice Awards. Food vendors can submit their dishes for a chance to win the creative food contest.

the 2010s, one Arizona State Fair stand served deep-fried scorpions! Spaghetti ice cream debuted at the California State Fair in 2013. This dessert featured noodle-shaped ice cream strands and strawberry "spaghetti" sauce. The Arkansas State Fair serves deep-fried watermelon on a stick.

State fair food has also become more culturally diverse. Several stands at the State Fair of Texas serve sopapillas, a fried bread common in Mexican and Tex-Mex cuisine. In 2022, Union Hmong Kitchen opened at the Minnesota State Fair. The stand served rice and meat dishes featuring lemongrass, ginger, and other classic Hmong

Sweet Martha's Cookie Jar produces three million cookies a day during the Minnesota State Fair.

flavors. For some fairgoers, trying new and interesting foods is a state fair tradition. Modern state fairs preview new foods on social media before the fairs open. These previews allow people to plan which new creations they will try.

Old Favorites

New state fair foods can make a splash. But there are several classic state fair foods that remain popular year after year. These include corn dogs, funnel cakes, and cheese curds. Individual states have their own fair favorites. The pork chop on a stick is popular at the Iowa State Fair. At the Minnesota State Fair, people wait in long lines to buy buckets of miniature chocolate chip cookies from Sweet Martha's Cookie Jar.

> One of the Wisconsin State Fair's most popular food items is the Original Cream Puff. It has been sold there since 1924. About 350,000 to 400,000 cream puffs are made each year.

STATE FAIR TRADITIONS

Each state fair has its own traditions. Learn about some of the most unique traditions across the 50 states!

Minnesota

Since 1954, the Minnesota State Fair has crowned a new Princess Kay of the Milky Way. Princess Kay is an ambassador for Minnesota's dairy farmers. She teaches people about dairy farming practices. Each Princess Kay's likeness is also carved in butter!

Texas

Since 1952, the "Big Tex" cowboy statue has greeted guests at the State Fair of Texas. The statue is more than 50 feet (15.2 m) tall. It can also talk!

The Big E

The Big E is a state fair for six states. They are Massachusetts, Maine, Vermont, New Hampshire, Connecticut, and Rhode Island. Each state has its own building along the fair's Avenue of States where fairgoers can buy food and products related to that state.

Mississippi

Since the 1950s, the Biscuit Booth at the Mississippi State Fair has served fairgoers free biscuits. Each one is handmade and served with syrup. In 2022, volunteers at the booth gave away nearly 74,000 biscuits!

Many state fairs that reopened in 2021 included COVID-19 vaccination tents and handwashing and sanitizing stations. Visitors were also encouraged to wear masks.

Chapter 6

WHAT'S NEXT?

Most state fairs had high attendance during the early 2000s, regularly welcoming millions of attendees. But in the 2020s, some fairs faced financial uncertainty. In 2020, many state fairs were canceled because of the COVID-19 pandemic. The pandemic also caused low attendance at many fairs in 2021. So there was less revenue to help improve and maintain state fairgrounds.

In addition, food vendors rely on strong sales to continue operating their businesses. Without enough revenue, future state fairs could be at risk of closing. However, vendors and fairgoers remained optimistic that state fairs would bounce back after the pandemic.

Big and Booming

In 2022, many state fairs were very well-attended. The 2022 State Fair of Texas welcomed more than 2.5 million visitors over 24 days. The same year, the Minnesota State Fair had more than 1.8 million visitors over 12 days. Nearly 250,000 people attended the fair on its busiest day. These two state fairs were the most popular in the country.

State Fairs Then and Now

State fairs have been part of American culture for more than 150 years. During that time, they have expanded to include new attractions, exhibits, foods, and more. Many state fairs have also recently adopted new technology, such as mobile apps. The apps allow fairgoers to view fairground maps, event schedules, and vendors from their phones.

So many people attend the Iowa State Fair that it can be difficult to walk around due to the crowds.

For decades, state fairs have offered both classic charm and constant change. They keep old traditions alive while establishing new ones. In 2022, only 1 percent of Americans lived on a farm. But state fairs still allow Americans from all backgrounds to learn about farming's importance.

State fairs have something for everyone. They are places to learn and try new things. They are also places that connect people to tradition and the past. Who knows what state fairs will introduce in the future? But they are sure to remain an important reflection of American culture.

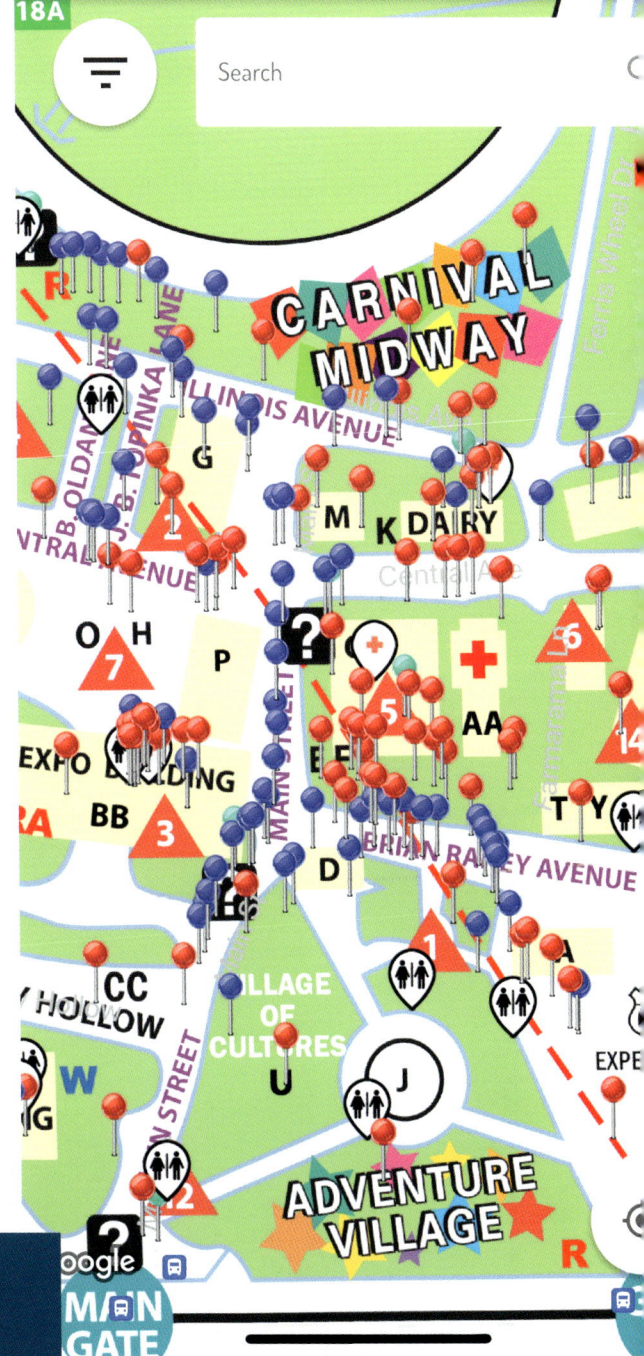

The Illinois State Fair app includes an interactive map. Users can search for specific events or vendors.

MAKE AMERICANA!

What can you create that is inspired by state fairs? Start by thinking about your favorite state fair foods, attractions, and historical themes. Then put your imagination to work!

Food on a stick is a modern state fair staple. Bust out a skewer. Then try turning one of your favorite foods into a fun, portable meal or snack! You could make a sandwich on a stick, pizza on a stick, chocolate-dipped fruit on a stick, and more.

Carve your own "butter" sculpture out of yellow clay! Use your state for inspiration. What state-related animal, industry, or landmark could you make?

Use cardboard, ribbon, glitter, paper, and other craft supplies to **make your own blue ribbon**!

TIMELINE

1810
Elkanah Watson organizes a livestock fair in Berkshire County, Massachusetts. It is the precursor to American state fairs.

1841
The first state fair is held in New York.

LATE 1800s–EARLY 1900s
Many state fairs move to permanent fairgrounds. This allows the fairs to expand in size and scope.

1940
Only 30 percent of Americans are farmers. Still, farming remains an important part of the state fair experience.

2020
Many state fairs are canceled because of the COVID-19 pandemic.

1942
The corn dog debuts at the State Fair of Texas.

2022
The State Fair of Texas welcomes 2.5 million visitors over 24 days. The Minnesota State Fair has 1.8 million attendees over 12 days.

GLOSSARY

architect—a person who plans and designs buildings.

carousel—a platform that turns and has seats and animal figures that people can sit on. Also called a merry-go-round.

category—a group of people or things that are similar in some way.

cuisine—a way or style of cooking food.

debut—a first appearance or to make a first appearance.

duration—how long something lasts.

eco-friendly—something that does not cause harm to the environment.

genetic—relating to or involving genes.

grandstand—a seating area for spectators at a racecourse or stadium.

Hmong—relating to people and culture from southeastern China and the northern parts of Vietnam, Laos, and Thailand.

inception—an act or instance of beginning.

muggy—warm and humid.

optimistic—looking upon actions or events in the most favorable or positive way.

pandemic—an outbreak of a disease that spreads quickly throughout the world.

parachutist—a person who jumps out of an aircraft and uses a specially designed cloth called a parachute to fall slowly to the ground.

showcase—to exhibit something to try to get others to like it.

suburban—related to a town, village, or community just outside a city.

technique—a method or style in which something is done.

textile—a woven fabric or cloth.

trapeze—a high, swinging bar that acrobats perform tricks on, usually at a circus.

urban—of or relating to a city.

vendor—someone who sells things.

ONLINE RESOURCES

To learn more about state fairs, please visit **abdobooklinks.com** or scan this QR code. These links are routinely monitored and updated to provide the most current information available.

INDEX

A
agriculture, 5-7, 9-12, 14, 17, 23-24, 26-27
animals, 5-7, 9-14, 17, 24-27, 43
Arizona State Fair, 34
Arkansas State Fair, 34
attractions, 5-6, 18, 20, 32, 40, 42

B
Berkshire Agricultural Society, 11
Big E, The, 37
buildings, 5-6, 12, 17, 24, 29, 31, 33, 37
butter sculptures, 5, 36, 43

C
California State Fair, 34
concerts, 6, 18-19
contests, 6, 27-28
county fairs, 12
COVID-19, 39
crops, 7, 9-11, 12, 14, 25
culture, 7, 34, 40-41

E
education, 7, 9, 12, 14, 17, 24-26, 29, 36, 41
environment, 7, 29
exhibitions, 10, 15, 25
exhibits, 17, 29, 40

F
fairgrounds, 6, 13, 17-19, 31, 39-40
food, 6-7, 9, 28, 31-35, 37, 39-40, 42
4-H, 26-27
Future Farmers of America (FFA), 26-27

G
grandstands, 18-19

I
Industrial Revolution, 9
Iowa State Fair, 13, 18-19, 35

M
Michigan State Fair, 13
midways, 5, 19-21
Minnesota State Fair, 13, 21, 29, 33-36, 39
Mississippi State Fair, 37

N
New York State Agricultural Society, 12
New York State Fair, 12-13, 17, 29

O
Ohio State Fair, 5

R
ribbons, 28, 43
rides, 5-6, 17, 19, 21

S
St. Louis World's Fair, 32
State Fair of Texas, 33-34, 36, 39-40
Sweet Martha's Cookie Jar, 35

T
technology, 7, 9, 12, 14, 21, 29, 40
Tom Thumb mini donuts, 33
traditions, 5, 7, 31, 35-37, 41

U
Union Hmong Kitchen, 34

W
Watson, Elkanah, 10-11
Wisconsin State Fair, 19